D0948671

Simple Machine Science

# Levers

**By Dwayne Stilwell**

 **Gareth Stevens**
Publishing

Please visit our website, www.garethstevens.com. For a free color catalog of all our high-quality books, call toll free 1-800-542-2595 or fax 1-877-542-2596.

Library of Congress Cataloging-in-Publication Data

Stilwell, Dwayne, author.
 Levers / Dwayne Stilwell.
     pages ; cm. — (Simple machine science)
 Includes bibliographical references and index.
 ISBN 978-1-4339-8137-1 (paperback)
 ISBN 978-1-4339-8138-8 (6-pack)
 ISBN 978-1-4339-8136-4 (library binding)
 1.  Levers—Juvenile literature.  I. Title.
 TJ147.S755 2013
 621.8—dc23

                                             2012019733

Published in 2013 by
**Gareth Stevens Publishing**
111 East 14th Street, Suite 349
New York, NY 10003

Copyright © 2013 Gareth Stevens Publishing

Designer: Katelyn E. Reynolds
Editor: Greg Roza

Photo credits: Cover, p. 1 Cenk Ertekin/Shutterstock.com; pp. 3–24 (background graphics) mike.irwin/Shutterstock.com; pp. 5, 17 (tongs, bottle opener), 19 (stapler, pliers), 21 iStockphoto/Thinkstock.com; p. 7 George F. Mobley/National Geographic/Getty Images; p. 9 Andrew Green/Getty Images; pp. 11, 17 (scissors) Hemera/Thinkstock.com; p. 13 © iStockphoto.com/Don Nichols; p. 15 Image Source/Thinkstock.com; p. 19 (fishing pole) Stockbyte/Thinkstock.com.

Printed in the United States of America

CPSIA compliance information: Batch #CW13GS: For further information contact Gareth Stevens, New York, New York at 1-800-542-2595.

# Contents

**Boldface** words appear in the glossary.

## What's a Lever?

Levers are used to lift or move heavy loads with little effort. Levers come in many shapes and sizes, but they're usually long. The longer a lever, the less effort it takes to lift or move a heavy load.

5

## Load and Effort

This man is using a wooden pole to move a heavy log. The pole is the lever. The log is the load. To move the load, the man uses effort to push down on the end of the lever.

7

# What's a Fulcrum?

All levers need a fulcrum. This is the part the lever rests on. The fulcrum allows the lever to **pivot**, or move in different directions. The fulcrum is in different places depending on the class, or type, of lever.

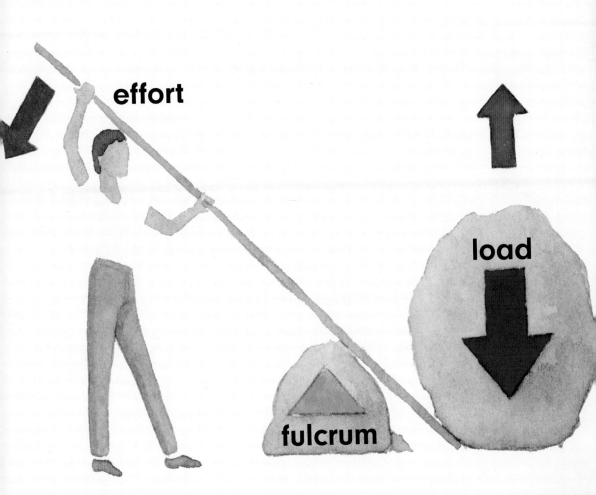

effort

load

fulcrum

9

# Class One Lever

A seesaw is a class one lever. A seesaw's fulcrum is in the middle. The person pushing down on one end of the lever is the effort. The person going up on the other side is the load.

load

fulcrum

effort

11

## Class Two Lever

With a class two lever, the fulcrum is on one end and the load is in the middle. A **wheelbarrow** is a class two lever. The wheel is the fulcrum. A person lifts the handles to move the load.

load

effort

fulcrum

13

# Class Three Lever

The fulcrum is on one end of a class three lever, and the load is on the other end. A shovel is a class three lever. You hold the end of the shovel (fulcrum) and pull up on the middle to dig up some dirt.

fulcrum

effort

load

15

## In the Home

Your house is loaded with levers! Scissors are class one levers. Bottle openers are class two levers. **Tongs** are class three levers. Life would be very different without these levers in our homes.

scissors

bottle
opener

tongs

17

## At Work with Levers

Many people use levers at their job every day. **Pliers** are class one levers. Staplers are class two levers. Fishing poles are class three levers. Without levers, many people wouldn't be able to do their job.

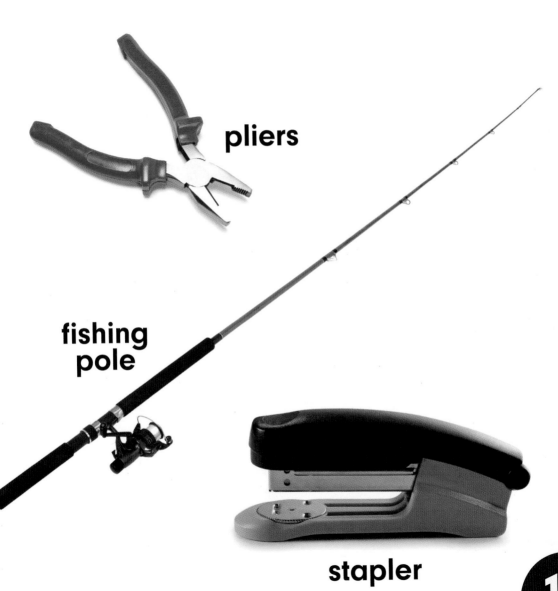

**pliers**

**fishing pole**

**stapler**

19

# Levers Inside You

We can find levers all around us, but they're also inside our bodies. Our bones are levers! They work like all three classes of levers to help us move and lift things. Levers really are everywhere!

# Levers in Your World

| lever | how it works | examples |
|-------|-------------|----------|
| class one | fulcrum is in the middle | seesaw, scissors, pliers |
| class two | fulcrum is on one end, load is in the middle | wheelbarrow, stapler, bottle opener |
| class three | fulcrum is on one end, load is on the other end | shovel, tongs, fishing pole |

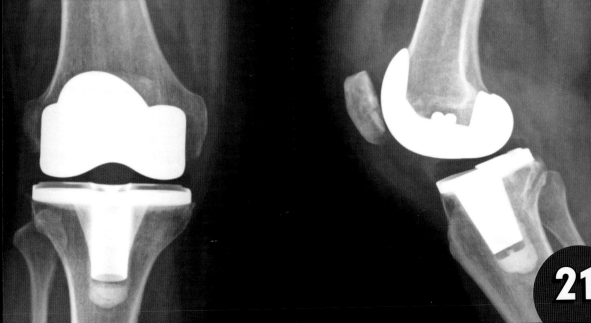

# Glossary

**pivot:** to move around a center point, such as a fulcrum

**pliers:** a tool used to grip or squeeze things

**tongs:** a tool with two arms used to hold or pick up things

**wheelbarrow:** a tool that has a wheel, handles, and a place to hold and move things

# For More Information

## Books

Dahl, Michael. *Scoop, Seesaw, and Raise: A Book About Levers.* Minneapolis, MN: Picture Window Books, 2006.

Gosman, Gillian. *Levers in Action.* New York, NY: PowerKids Press, 2011.

Volpe, Karen. *Get to Know Levers.* New York, NY: Crabtree Publishing, 2009.

## Websites

**Levers**
*www.technologystudent.com/forcmom/lever1.htm*
This website includes diagrams to help readers understand the differences between the three classes of levers.

**Levers: Simple Machines**
*www.enchantedlearning.com/physics/machines/Levers.shtml*
Learn more about levers and see more examples of the three classes.

**Simple Machines**
*www.msichicago.org/fileadmin/Activities/Games/simple_machines/*
Learn more about levers and other simple machines by playing a fun online game.

# Index